CONTENTS

Italy Unlocked: A Short Guide to Travelling and Selling in Italy   1
Chapter 1: The Geography and Culture of Italy   6
Chapter 2: The Logistics of Travelling in Italy   13
Chapter 3: Setting Up Your Business in Italy   20
Chapter 4: What to Sell in Italy: Market Insights   26
Chapter 5: Selling Industrial Products and Services in Italy   32
Chapter 6: Selling at Markets and Fairs in Italy   40
Chapter 7: Selling Online in Italy   47
Chapter 8: Marketing Strategies for Italian Consumers   54
Chapter 9: Navigating Cultural and Business Etiquette   61
Chapter 10: Conclusion: Embrace the Opportunity in Italy   68
About The Author   75

ITALY UNLOCKED:
A SHORT GUIDE TO TRAVELLING AND SELLING IN ITALY

J K Lewis

Introduction: Why Italy is the Perfect Place for Entrepreneurs and Travelers

Italy is a country that stirs the imagination, known for its timeless beauty, cultural heritage, and passion for design, fashion, and gastronomy. With a rich history dating back to the Roman Empire and a vibrant present as a global leader in art, fashion, and craftsmanship, Italy attracts millions of visitors each year. But beyond its appeal as a tourist destination, Italy also presents vast opportunities for entrepreneurs looking to sell their products in a dynamic and discerning market.

From the cobblestone streets of Florence to the fashion houses of Milan, Italy's markets are a perfect blend of tradition and modernity. Italian consumers are known for their appreciation of quality, craftsmanship, and authenticity. They value products that have a story behind them, whether it's a handwoven scarf from a Tuscan artisan or an eco-friendly leather bag designed in Rome. This makes Italy an ideal place for entrepreneurs who are passionate about their products and who want to connect with customers who value authenticity.

Italy's thriving economy is built on the strength of its small and medium-sized businesses, known as piccole e medie imprese (PMI), which are the backbone of its economy. Many of these businesses are family-owned and operate in sectors such as fashion, food, art, and craftsmanship. If you have a product that embodies the qualities of Italian life - attention to detail, beauty, and sustainability - Italy provides fertile ground for success.

Whether you're looking to sell luxury items, artisanal goods, or food products, Italy offers a receptive market. The Italian consumer is sophisticated, often looking for products that blend tradition with innovation. Italians are known for supporting local businesses, but they also embrace international brands that align with their tastes and values.

Travelling and Selling in Italy

For the entrepreneurial traveller, Italy offers a unique opportunity to combine business with the joy of exploring one of the world's most beautiful countries. Travelling through Italy is not only a chance to immerse yourself in its rich cultural heritage but also to tap into the country's diverse regional markets. Each region in Italy has its own distinct character, consumer preferences, and seasonal events, from the fashion-forward streets of Milan to the artisanal markets of Sicily.

Italy's vibrant market culture is one of its most appealing features for travelling entrepreneurs. Markets and fairs take place across the country, offering sellers a direct way to connect with consumers. Whether it's selling handcrafted goods in Tuscany's piazzas or showcasing your products at one of Rome's bustling markets, Italy allows you to engage with customers face-to-face, build relationships, and grow your brand organically.

What You'll Learn in This Guide

This book is designed to provide you with everything you need to know about travelling and selling in Italy. Whether you're just starting out as an entrepreneur or you're looking to expand your business into the Italian market, this guide will give you the insights and strategies to succeed. Here's what you'll learn:

- **Understanding Italian Regions and Consumer Behaviour:** Italy's 20 regions each have their own unique culture, consumer habits, and market opportunities. You'll learn how to navigate the differences between northern, central, and southern

Italy, as well as how to tailor your products to regional preferences.

- **Travel Logistics and Selling on the Road:** Discover how to travel efficiently between cities and regions in Italy, manage your inventory, and find accommodations that support your business needs. Whether you're using Italy's high-speed trains or renting a car to visit rural markets, this guide will help you plan your journey.

- **Setting Up Your Business in Italy:** Learn how to legally establish your business in Italy, manage taxes, and ensure you comply with local regulations. From registering for a VAT number to understanding Italian business structures, this guide will take you step by step through the process.

- **Selling at Markets and Fairs:** Italy's markets are legendary, and selling at these venues provides a fantastic opportunity to connect with consumers. You'll learn how to apply for market stalls, set up an attractive booth, and engage with Italian customers to maximise your sales.

- **E-Commerce and Online Selling in Italy:** In addition to traditional markets, Italy's e-commerce sector is growing. This guide will show you how to build a successful online store, optimise it for Italian customers, and manage logistics for shipping across the country.

- **Marketing to Italian Consumers:** Italians are influenced by aesthetics, quality, and storytelling. You'll discover how to craft marketing messages that resonate with Italian buyers, from social media strategies to influencer partnerships and email marketing.

- **Navigating Italian Business Etiquette:** Italian business culture places a strong emphasis on relationships and trust. This guide will teach you how to conduct business meetings, negotiate deals, and build long-term relationships with clients and partners in Italy.

Who This Guide is For

Whether you're an artisan selling handcrafted goods, a fashion designer looking to break into the Italian market, or an entrepreneur interested in selling gourmet food or eco-friendly products, this guide is for you. It's designed for anyone who dreams of combining their love for travel with the adventure of building a successful business in Italy.

If you're ready to embrace the opportunity, dive into the rich culture, and navigate Italy's unique marketplace, this guide will provide you with the tools and insights you need to succeed. With careful planning, a deep appreciation for the Italian market, and a passion for your products, you can unlock the potential of travelling and selling in Italy.

CHAPTER 1: THE GEOGRAPHY AND CULTURE OF ITALY

Italy is a land of extraordinary diversity, where each region has its own distinct culture, traditions, and economy. From the bustling streets of Milan to the rolling vineyards of Tuscany and the coastal beauty of Sicily, every part of Italy offers unique opportunities for entrepreneurs. Understanding Italy's regional differences and consumer behaviour is essential for selling successfully in this vibrant market. This chapter explores the geographical and cultural nuances of Italy's regions and provides insights into how to tailor your business approach to each one.

1.1 Overview of Italy's Regions (Regioni)

Italy is divided into 20 administrative regions, each with its own unique identity, local products, and consumer preferences. These regions can be broadly categorised into northern, central, and southern areas, each with distinct market opportunities.

Lombardy (Lombardia)
- **Capital:** Milan
- **Why It's Important:** Lombardy is Italy's most economically developed region and a global centre for fashion, finance, and business. Milan, its capital, is renowned for its luxury goods, innovative design, and major fashion events, making it a prime destination for selling fashion and high-end products.

- **Key Cities**: Milan, Bergamo, Brescia
- **Market Insights**: Milan is known as the fashion capital of the world, hosting **Milan Fashion Week** and various luxury trade shows. High-end goods, from fashion to jewellery, are well-suited to this market. Outside Milan, cities like Bergamo and Brescia offer strong markets for traditional crafts and artisanal products, where the focus is more on craftsmanship and authenticity.

Tuscany (Toscana)

- **Capital**: Florence
- **Why It's Important**: Tuscany is globally recognised for its contributions to art, culture, and wine. Florence, the heart of the Renaissance, is a cultural hub where tourists flock for its artistic heritage and craftsmanship. Tuscany is also known for its agricultural products, including wine, olive oil, and leather goods.
- **Key Cities**: Florence, Pisa, Siena
- **Market Insights**: In Florence, handmade products such as leather goods, ceramics, and textiles are popular, with tourists seeking authentic, local craftsmanship. The region's strong agricultural sector creates opportunities for selling gourmet foods and organic products. Wine-related goods and high-end artisanal products also do well in this region, where local pride in tradition and craftsmanship is strong.

Veneto

- **Capital**: Venice
- **Why It's Important**: Veneto is a region rich in history, art, and industry. Venice, the capital, is one of the most visited cities in the world, known for its unique markets selling artisanal goods like Murano glass and Burano lace. Veneto is also a major manufacturing centre, producing everything from textiles to luxury goods.

- **Key Cities**: Venice, Verona, Padua
- **Market Insights**: Venice offers strong opportunities for selling to tourists who are interested in unique, high-quality items such as artisanal glassware, jewellery, and decorative crafts. Verona and Padua, on the other hand, have more local-focused markets where fashion, beauty products, and lifestyle goods perform well.

Sicily (Sicilia)
- **Capital**: Palermo
- **Why It's Important**: Sicily is a cultural and culinary gem with a strong agricultural tradition. The island is famous for its high-quality olive oil, citrus fruits, and wines. Its growing tourism industry provides a large market for handcrafted products, ceramics, and gourmet foods.
- **Key Cities**: Palermo, Catania, Syracuse
- **Market Insights**: Sicily's markets are known for their focus on local, artisanal goods such as ceramics, jewellery, and gourmet foods. Palermo and Catania are bustling cities with vibrant street markets where entrepreneurs can sell traditional crafts, while smaller towns offer strong demand for local food products, organic produce, and handmade goods.

Lazio
- **Capital**: Rome
- **Why It's Important**: Lazio is home to Rome, Italy's capital and one of the world's most historically significant cities. As a global tourism hub, Rome offers vast opportunities for selling to both international visitors and locals.
- **Key Cities**: Rome, Frosinone, Latina
- **Market Insights**: Rome has a diverse consumer base,

making it an ideal place for selling everything from fashion and art to antiques and gourmet food. Markets such as **Campo de' Fiori** and **Porta Portese** are excellent venues for selling handmade crafts, fashion items, and food products to a mix of locals and tourists. Rome's markets offer a unique blend of tradition and modernity, with opportunities for entrepreneurs in various industries.

1.2 Urban vs. Rural Markets

Italy's diverse landscape means that urban and rural markets offer different opportunities for entrepreneurs. While cities like Milan, Rome, and Florence provide access to fashion-forward, trend-conscious consumers, rural areas are ideal for selling artisanal goods and products with a local connection.

Urban Markets

- **Consumer Profile**: Urban consumers in Italy are typically affluent, trend-conscious, and have a higher disposable income. They are drawn to luxury items, cutting-edge fashion, and innovative products. Cities like Milan and Rome, in particular, are hubs for high-end shopping, where consumers seek both luxury brands and unique, one-of-a-kind products.

- **Competition**: The urban marketplace is competitive, especially in cities like Milan, where fashion and design dominate. To succeed, entrepreneurs need to stand out through strong branding, innovative product offerings, and high-quality customer service.

- **Market Opportunities**: Urban markets are ideal for high-end fashion, artisanal products, gourmet foods, and tech innovations. Pop-up shops, designer markets, and seasonal events are common in cities like Milan, Florence, and Rome, offering great opportunities for entrepreneurs to showcase their products.

Rural Markets

- **Consumer Profile**: Consumers in rural areas tend to value tradition, local craftsmanship, and quality over trends. They are more price-conscious but also deeply loyal to local producers and artisans. Products that reflect the region's cultural heritage or are tied to agricultural practices perform well in these markets.
- **Competition**: Rural markets often have fewer competitors, but consumers have high expectations for authenticity and quality. Selling in rural areas requires a deep understanding of local traditions and consumer preferences.
- **Market Opportunities**: Artisanal crafts, local foods, and handmade goods are the best-suited products for rural markets. In regions like Tuscany, Sicily, and Umbria, there is a strong market for organic produce, handcrafted items, and goods that reflect the region's history and culture.

1.3 Understanding Italian Consumer Culture

Italian consumers are known for their love of quality, beauty, and tradition. Whether they are purchasing fashion, food, or home goods, Italian buyers expect products to meet high standards of design and craftsmanship. To succeed in Italy, it's crucial to understand the values that drive consumer decisions.

Quality and Craftsmanship

Italian consumers place a high value on quality and craftsmanship, especially for fashion, home goods, and artisanal products. Whether buying a handbag or a bottle of wine, Italians prefer well-made items that reflect a strong tradition of craftsmanship and attention to detail.

- **Highlight Craftsmanship**: Emphasise the quality and artisanal aspects of your products. Italian consumers appreciate products with a clear story behind them, particularly those made with care and precision.

Sustainability and Eco-Consciousness

Sustainability is becoming increasingly important to Italian consumers, particularly in urban areas. There is growing demand for eco-friendly products, organic goods, and items made with sustainable materials.

- **Sustainable Products**: Whether it's organic food, eco-friendly fashion, or sustainably sourced crafts, products with a strong environmental message are increasingly popular. Highlighting your commitment to sustainability can give your products a competitive edge, especially with younger consumers.

Tradition Meets Innovation

While Italians value tradition, they also appreciate innovation that enhances their daily lives. Combining modern convenience with traditional design or artisanal craftsmanship can appeal to consumers who want the best of both worlds.

- **Balancing Tradition and Modernity**: Products that combine traditional elements with modern functionality—such as tech-enhanced fashion or artisanal goods with a contemporary twist—are likely to resonate well with Italian buyers.

Aesthetics and Design

Italians have a deep appreciation for beauty and aesthetics in all aspects of life. Products that are stylish, elegant, and thoughtfully designed are highly valued, whether they are clothing, home decor, or everyday items.

- **Focus on Visual Appeal**: Ensure your products are not only functional but also aesthetically pleasing. Packaging, branding, and product presentation are crucial elements that influence purchasing decisions in Italy.

Chapter 1 - Summary
Italy's geographical and cultural diversity offers a wide range of opportunities for entrepreneurs. Whether you're selling luxury fashion in Milan, handmade crafts in Florence, or gourmet food in Sicily, understanding the regional distinctions and consumer preferences will be key to your success. Italian consumers value quality, craftsmanship, and sustainability, and they appreciate products with a strong connection to local traditions. By tailoring your offerings to these values, you can carve out a niche in this highly discerning market.

CHAPTER 2: THE LOGISTICS OF TRAVELLING IN ITALY

Italy's extensive transportation network and diverse landscape make it an ideal country for entrepreneurs looking to travel and sell their products. Whether you're exploring bustling urban centres or charming rural villages, getting around Italy efficiently is key to managing your business. This chapter covers the best transportation options, accommodations for entrepreneurs, and practical tips for organising and transporting your goods.

2.1 Transportation Options for Travelers

Italy offers a variety of transportation options, allowing you to move between cities and regions with ease. Depending on your destination and business needs, you can choose from high-speed trains, rental cars, buses, or local transportation systems.

Train Travel: High-Speed and Regional Trains

- **Frecciarossa and Italo (High-Speed Trains)**: Italy's high-speed trains, such as **Frecciarossa** and **Italo**, connect major cities like Milan, Rome, Florence, and Naples. These trains are fast, reliable, and comfortable, making them a great option for travelling between large cities. The trip from Milan to Rome, for example, takes around 3 hours. High-speed trains are an efficient choice for entrepreneurs needing to travel between urban centres while carrying smaller amounts of inventory.

- **Regional Trains**: For travelling to smaller towns and rural areas, regional trains (operated by **Trenitalia**) provide a more affordable, though slower, option. These trains connect major cities to smaller towns in regions like Tuscany, Umbria, and Sicily. Regional trains are ideal for reaching markets in rural areas or visiting smaller, local fairs.

Car Rentals: Flexibility for Reaching Remote Markets

- **Renting a Car**: Renting a car gives you the flexibility to explore rural areas and remote markets where public transportation may not be readily available. Car rentals are widely available through companies like **Hertz**, **Avis**, and **Europcar**, with pickup locations at major airports and cities across Italy. For transporting larger amounts of inventory, consider renting a van or cargo vehicle.

- **Driving in Italy**: Italy's roads are well-maintained, especially the highways (known as **autostrade**), which connect major cities. However, be aware that many highways are tolled, and speed limits are strictly enforced. Renting a car is the best option if you plan to visit rural markets or transport larger amounts of goods between cities and smaller towns.

Public Transportation in Cities

- **Metro and Tram Systems**: In large cities like Rome, Milan, and Turin, public transportation systems are reliable and convenient. The **ATM** network in Milan and **ATAC** in Rome provide metro, tram, and bus services that make it easy to get around within city limits. If you're visiting multiple markets in a city, public transportation can be a cost-effective and fast way to travel.

- **Buses**: For smaller towns and rural areas, buses are the primary mode of public transportation. Italy's bus networks are extensive, with services connecting cities, towns, and rural regions. For example, the **SITA** bus network covers much of Tuscany, making it a good option for entrepreneurs visiting rural markets.

2.2 Accommodation for Travelling Entrepreneurs

Choosing the right accommodation while travelling for business is essential for staying productive and managing your inventory. Italy offers a wide range of accommodation to suit different budgets and business needs.

Short-Term Rentals (Airbnb, Vrbo)

- **Airbnb and Vrbo**: Short-term rental platforms like **Airbnb** and **Vrbo** are ideal for entrepreneurs who need flexibility and space. Many properties offer larger apartments or houses with kitchens and storage areas, allowing you to manage your inventory and set up a temporary workspace. If you're staying in a region for an extended period, renting an apartment or house can provide the convenience and comfort needed for running your business.

Business Hotels

- **Hotel Chains**: Business hotels such as **NH Hotels**, **Best Western**, and **Novotel** can be found throughout Italy, especially in larger cities like Milan, Rome, and Florence. These hotels offer amenities such as Wi-Fi, business centres, and meeting rooms, making them ideal for entrepreneurs on the go. Staying in a business hotel ensures that you have access to the resources needed for staying connected and managing your business remotely.

- **Extended-Stay Hotels**: For longer stays, consider booking an extended-stay hotel that offers apartment-style rooms with kitchenettes and laundry services. These hotels are a comfortable option for entrepreneurs who need to stay in one location for an extended period while managing their inventory and operations.

Hostels

- **Budget-Friendly Hostels**: Hostels in Italy, particularly in cities like Florence, Venice, and Rome, offer a budget-friendly accommodation option. Many hostels now provide private rooms in addition to shared dormitories, offering privacy and security for your belongings. While hostels may not offer the same amenities as business hotels, they can be a great option for short stays, especially if you're travelling light.

Agriturismi (Farm Stays)

- **Agriturismi**: Agriturismi, or farm stays, are a unique and culturally immersive accommodation option found in rural areas like Tuscany, Umbria, and Sicily. These farm stays often offer beautiful countryside settings and the opportunity to experience Italian rural life. They can be ideal for entrepreneurs visiting regional markets and fairs in rural areas while enjoying a more relaxed environment.

2.3 Organising the Transport of Goods

Managing your inventory and transporting your goods efficiently is essential for success as a travelling entrepreneur in Italy. Whether you're selling at local markets or fulfilling online orders, having a reliable logistics plan is crucial.

Shipping Goods via Couriers

- **Poste Italiane**: Italy's national postal service, **Poste Italiane**, offers reliable and affordable shipping options for businesses. Their services include **Pacco Ordinario** (standard shipping) and **Posta Celere** (express delivery).

- Poste Italiane is a good option for sending small packages or fulfilling e-commerce orders domestically and internationally.
- **Private Couriers**: For larger shipments or time-sensitive deliveries, private couriers like **DHL**, **UPS**, and **FedEx** offer fast, reliable services throughout Italy and beyond. These couriers are ideal if you're handling larger volumes of goods or need to ship products quickly to customers across Italy.

Transporting Goods Yourself

- **Rental Vehicles**: If you're travelling between markets or fairs and carrying large amounts of inventory, renting a van or cargo vehicle is often the most practical solution. Rental companies such as **Europcar** and **Avis** offer vehicles suited for transporting goods, and many of Italy's markets have easy access for setting up stalls and unloading products.
- **Packing and Display**: Proper packing is essential for protecting your goods while travelling. Invest in sturdy packaging, crates, or boxes to prevent damage during transport. Portable display materials such as folding tables, shelves, and banners can also help you set up an attractive and professional stall at markets.

Shipping Products to Customers

For entrepreneurs selling online or managing an e-commerce business, ensuring smooth and reliable shipping for customer orders is critical.

- **E-Commerce Shipping Solutions**: Platforms like **ShipStation** and **SendCloud** are designed to simplify the shipping process. These platforms allow you to manage orders, compare shipping rates, and print shipping labels from various couriers, streamlining your logistics.

- **Fulfillment Centres**: If you're selling large volumes or prefer not to travel with your inventory, partnering with a fulfilment centre in Italy can be an efficient solution. Fulfilment centres store your products and handle packing and shipping on your behalf, allowing you to focus on marketing and growing your business.

2.4 Managing Business on the Go

Running a business while travelling requires organisation and access to reliable tools and resources. From managing payments to staying connected, here's how you can keep your operations running smoothly while on the move.

Internet Access

Having reliable internet access is essential for managing your business. Italy has excellent mobile network coverage, and providers like **TIM**, **Vodafone**, and **WindTre** offer prepaid SIM cards with data plans, allowing you to stay connected wherever you travel. Wi-Fi is widely available in hotels, cafes, and co-working spaces throughout Italy.

Payment Processing

When selling at markets or pop-up shops, offering mobile payment options is crucial for ensuring smooth transactions. Popular payment processors in Italy include:

- **SumUp**: SumUp allows you to accept credit and debit card payments via a mobile card reader, making it perfect for market vendors and small business owners who need to process payments on the go.
- **Zettle by PayPal**: Formerly known as **iZettle**, this mobile payment system integrates with PayPal and offers card readers that connect to your smartphone or tablet, providing a seamless payment experience.

Invoicing and Accounting

Managing your finances while travelling is key to staying organised. Several software solutions and apps are designed to help entrepreneurs track expenses, send invoices, and manage taxes while on the move:

- **QuickBooks**: This popular accounting software allows you to manage invoices, track expenses, and monitor cash flow, all from your smartphone or laptop.
- **Fatture in Cloud**: Designed specifically for the Italian market, **Fatture in Cloud** simplifies invoicing and tax compliance for entrepreneurs, making it easy to issue invoices and track payments while on the go.

Chapter 2 - Summary

Travelling in Italy as an entrepreneur offers a wealth of opportunities, but it also requires careful planning and logistics. Whether you're using high-speed trains, renting a vehicle, or relying on couriers for shipping, Italy's infrastructure makes it relatively easy to move between markets and manage your business. Choosing the right accommodations, staying connected, and organising your goods efficiently are key to ensuring a smooth business operation while travelling. With the right tools and strategies in place, you can successfully navigate Italy's diverse landscape and take advantage of its vibrant marketplace.

CHAPTER 3: SETTING UP YOUR BUSINESS IN ITALY

Italy offers a wealth of opportunities for entrepreneurs, but establishing a business in the country requires navigating its legal and regulatory environment. Understanding the local business structures, tax requirements, and legal obligations is crucial for ensuring that your venture runs smoothly. Whether you're looking to sell in local markets, open a storefront, or run an online business, this chapter will guide you through the steps to setting up a business in Italy.

3.1 Legal Framework for Selling in Italy

The Italian legal system offers several business structures tailored to different types of entrepreneurs. Choosing the right structure for your business is important, as it affects your taxes, liabilities, and administrative responsibilities.

Business Structures in Italy

Italy offers a range of legal business structures, from small sole proprietorships to more formal company models. Here are the most common structures for entrepreneurs:

- **Partita IVA (Individual Entrepreneur)**: This is the simplest and most common business structure for small businesses and freelancers. It allows individuals to operate as sole proprietors, offering a flexible option for those starting small. The **Partita IVA** (VAT number) is required to conduct any type of business in Italy, and it is used for tax purposes.
- **SRL (Società a Responsabilità Limitata)**: The **SRL** is a limited liability company structure, similar to an LLC in

other countries. It protects personal assets by separating them from the company's liabilities. An **SRL** is more complex to set up than a sole proprietorship, but it's a suitable option for entrepreneurs looking to scale their businesses or bring in partners.

- **SAS (Società in Accomandita Semplice)**: The **SAS** is a partnership structure that includes both general and limited partners. General partners manage the company and are liable for its debts, while limited partners contribute capital but are not involved in day-to-day operations. This structure is often used for family-run businesses or partnerships between investors.

- **SNC (Società in Nome Collettivo)**: The **SNC** is a general partnership in which all partners share equal responsibility for the company's debts and liabilities. It is suitable for small businesses where all partners are equally involved in management and operations.

Which Business Structure is Right for You?

- If you're starting as a solo entrepreneur or freelancer, the **Partita IVA** is the simplest option and allows you to manage your business with minimal paperwork.
- For businesses with multiple partners or those looking to scale and protect personal assets, an **SRL** offers limited liability and more formal governance.
- If you're entering a partnership with clear roles between managing and investing partners, consider an **SAS**.

Registering Your Business

Once you've chosen the appropriate business structure, the next step is to register your business with the relevant authorities. The registration process varies depending on the structure you select, but the general steps are as follows:

1. **Obtain a Partita IVA**: If you're setting up as an individual entrepreneur (Partita IVA), you'll need to apply for a VAT number. This can be done online through the **Agenzia delle Entrate** (Revenue Agency) or with the help of a commercialista (accountant).

2. **Register with the Chamber of Commerce**: If you're setting up an SRL or another formal structure, you'll need to register your business with the local **Camera di Commercio** (Chamber of Commerce). You will also need to submit the company's articles of incorporation and other required documents.

3. **Social Security Registration**: All business owners must register with the Italian social security system (**INPS**). Contributions vary depending on your business structure and income. Self-employed individuals with a Partita IVA will typically contribute a percentage of their income, while larger companies with employees will face more complex payroll obligations.

4. **Open a Business Bank Account**: It's essential to open a dedicated business bank account for managing your company's finances. Most Italian banks offer tailored services for small businesses and entrepreneurs. A separate account will make it easier to track income and expenses and comply with tax requirements.

3.2 Managing Taxes and VAT (IVA)

Taxes in Italy are a crucial part of doing business, and understanding your obligations is key to staying compliant. Italy has a complex tax system, which includes both income tax and VAT (IVA).

Understanding VAT (IVA)

- **What is VAT (IVA)?**: VAT, known as **IVA (Imposta sul Valore Aggiunto)** in Italy, is a consumption tax applied to most goods and services. The standard VAT rate is

22%, but there are reduced rates for certain products and services, such as food (4-10%) and cultural goods (10%).

- **Do You Need to Charge VAT?**: If you run a business that generates over a certain threshold in annual revenue, you must charge VAT on your sales. This threshold is currently set at €85,000 for businesses. However, even if you earn less than this amount, you may choose to opt into the VAT system. Once registered, you are required to add VAT to your sales, submit VAT returns, and pay the tax you collect to the government.

- **How to Register for VAT**: When you apply for your Partita IVA, you will automatically be registered for VAT if you meet the revenue requirements. If you opt to charge VAT on a voluntary basis, you'll need to register for VAT with the **Agenzia delle Entrate**.

Income Tax for Entrepreneurs

- **Income Tax for Partita IVA**: If you operate as an individual entrepreneur under the Partita IVA structure, your income is taxed based on a progressive income tax system. Tax rates vary depending on your income level, with higher earners paying a higher percentage. In addition to income tax, you will also be required to make social security contributions to **INPS**.

- **Corporate Tax for SRLs**: For businesses structured as SRLs or other formal entities, profits are subject to corporate tax (**IRES**). The standard corporate tax rate in Italy is 24%, though certain deductions and allowances may apply. Corporate entities are also subject to regional production tax (**IRAP**), which ranges from 3.9% to 4.8%, depending on the region.

Hiring an Accountant (Commercialista)

Given the complexities of Italy's tax system, it's highly recommended to hire a local accountant (**commercialista**) to help manage your finances. A commercialista can assist with VAT registration, tax filings, and social security contributions, ensuring that your business remains compliant with Italian law.

3.3 Compliance and Consumer Protection Laws

Italy has strict regulations regarding consumer rights, particularly for businesses selling to the public. Complying with these laws is crucial for maintaining trust with your customers and avoiding legal issues.

Right to Return (Diritto di Recesso)

- **Consumer Returns**: Italian law requires that customers have the right to return most goods purchased online or at a distance within 14 days of receipt. This is part of the EU's broader consumer protection laws, which apply in Italy. Be sure to include clear return policies on your website or in your sales materials, and make the process easy for customers to understand.

Warranties

- **Product Warranties**: Italian law mandates that products sold to consumers must come with a minimum two-year warranty against defects. This applies to both physical goods and digital products. As a seller, it's your responsibility to ensure that your products meet these standards and that you honour warranty claims promptly.

Product Safety and Labelling

- **Labelling Requirements**: Italian consumers expect transparency when it comes to product labelling, particularly for food and cosmetics. Ensure that your labels include all legally required information, such as ingredients, allergens, expiration dates, and the country of origin. Non-compliance with labelling requirements can result in fines or legal action.

Data Protection and GDPR

If you collect personal data from customers - whether for e-commerce sales, email newsletters, or customer accounts - you must comply with the **General Data Protection Regulation (GDPR)**, which applies throughout the EU. GDPR mandates that businesses protect personal data and provide transparency about how that data is used. Violations of GDPR can result in significant fines.

- **Privacy Policy**: Include a clear privacy policy on your website that explains how customer data is collected, stored, and used. Customers must also be able to opt out of data collection or unsubscribe from marketing communications.

Chapter 3 - Summary

Setting up a business in Italy requires careful planning and adherence to local regulations. Whether you're operating as an individual entrepreneur or forming a company, choosing the right business structure is critical for managing your taxes, liabilities, and administrative responsibilities. Understanding Italy's tax system, including VAT and income tax, and staying compliant with consumer protection laws, will help you establish a solid foundation for your business. With the right legal structure, financial management, and attention to customer rights, your business can thrive in the Italian marketplace.

CHAPTER 4: WHAT TO SELL IN ITALY: MARKET INSIGHTS

Italy is a country that takes pride in its culture, craftsmanship, and tradition. Italian consumers are highly discerning, with an eye for quality, design, and authenticity. Whether you're selling fashion, artisanal goods, gourmet food, or luxury products, understanding what resonates with the Italian market is key to success. This chapter will explore the best-selling product categories in Italy, seasonal and regional trends, and the growing demand for sustainability.

4.1 Best-Selling Products in Italy

Italy's rich culture, love for art and design, and deep-rooted traditions create a strong demand for certain types of products. From luxury fashion to locally crafted goods, here are the categories that thrive in the Italian marketplace.

Fashion and Apparel

Italy is one of the world's fashion capitals, known for its exquisite taste in clothing, shoes, and accessories. Fashion is a significant part of the Italian identity, and consumers are drawn to high-quality, stylish products.

- **What Sells**: Clothing, handbags, shoes, jewellery, and accessories are highly popular. Italian consumers appreciate both luxury fashion brands and smaller, independent designers offering unique or handmade items. Sustainable and eco-conscious fashion is also gaining popularity, particularly among younger, urban buyers.
- **Where to Sell**: Milan is the heart of Italy's fashion

industry and a great place to sell designer or high-end fashion products. Cities like Rome, Florence, and Venice also have strong fashion markets, with boutiques and pop-up stores providing ideal venues for showcasing your brand.

Artisanal and Handcrafted Goods

Italy has a long history of craftsmanship, and consumers value products that are handmade, authentic, and of high quality. This is especially true in regions like Tuscany, Sicily, and Umbria, where local crafts are a major part of the economy.

- **What Sells**: Handcrafted leather goods, ceramics, jewellery, textiles, and furniture are all popular with Italian consumers, particularly if they are made using traditional techniques. Products that are unique, customisable, or have a personal touch tend to perform well.

- **Where to Sell**: Artisanal markets, boutique stores, and local fairs are ideal places to sell handcrafted goods. In cities like Florence and Siena, which have a strong tradition of leather and ceramic craftsmanship, there is a constant demand for high-quality, locally made items.

Gourmet Food and Beverages

Italy is renowned for its culinary heritage, and gourmet food products have a dedicated market. Italians appreciate high-quality, artisanal food and are particularly passionate about local and organic produce.

- **What Sells**: Wine, olive oil, truffles, cheese, and pasta are staples in the gourmet food market. Organic and sustainably sourced foods are becoming increasingly popular, particularly among health-conscious consumers. Artisanal food products, such as handmade pasta or regional specialties, are also in high demand.

- **Where to Sell**: Food markets, gourmet food stores, and

online platforms catering to Italian food lovers are excellent venues for selling your products. Cities like Bologna, known as Italy's food capital, and regions like Tuscany and Sicily, where food traditions run deep, are ideal locations for food vendors.

Beauty and Wellness Products

The beauty and wellness sector is thriving in Italy, with consumers seeking out high-quality skincare, cosmetics, and wellness products. Italians are particularly interested in natural and organic beauty products.

- **What Sells**: Skincare products, organic cosmetics, essential oils, and wellness-related items are all popular in Italy. Italian consumers are increasingly looking for products that are eco-friendly, made from natural ingredients, and free from harmful chemicals.

- **Where to Sell**: Beauty products can be sold at specialty markets, health and wellness fairs, or through online platforms like **Ecco Verde**, which focuses on organic and natural beauty products.

Luxury Goods

Italy is known for its luxury market, especially in cities like Milan, Rome, and Florence. From fashion to home decor, Italians appreciate high-end, well-crafted products.

- **What Sells**: Luxury items such as designer handbags, high-end watches, fine jewellery, and upscale home decor are in high demand. Italian consumers expect premium quality and are willing to pay a premium for goods that offer sophistication and exclusivity.

- **Where to Sell**: Milan, the fashion capital, and Rome, with its historic elegance, are ideal places to sell luxury goods. Florence, known for its leather and artisanal goods, is also a great location for high-end products.

4.2 Seasonal and Regional Trends

Consumer demand in Italy is influenced by both regional preferences and seasonal trends. Understanding these factors can help you tailor your product offerings to match local tastes and capitalize on peak shopping periods.

Seasonal Trends

- **Christmas Markets (Mercatini di Natale)**: Christmas markets are hugely popular in Italy, particularly in northern regions like Trentino-Alto Adige. These markets attract both locals and tourists looking for holiday gifts, decorations, and festive food. Christmas markets are a perfect venue for selling artisanal goods, handcrafted ornaments, and seasonal food products.

- **Summer Tourism**: The summer months bring an influx of tourists to Italy's coastal regions, including the Amalfi Coast, Sardinia, and Sicily. These areas are ideal for selling beachwear, summer fashion, and locally crafted souvenirs. Coastal markets thrive on the tourist trade, with a particular demand for handmade goods and food specialties.

- **Harvest Festivals (Sagre)**: During the fall, many regions celebrate their agricultural heritage with harvest festivals known as **sagre**. These festivals focus on local produce like wine, chestnuts, and truffles, making them ideal venues for selling gourmet food products and locally made goods.

Regional Trends

- **Northern Italy**: In northern Italy, particularly in regions like Lombardy, Veneto, and Piedmont, there is a strong demand for luxury goods, fashion, and artisanal products. Milan is a global fashion hub, while Venice and

Verona are known for their strong tourism industries and focus on high-quality, locally made products.
- **Central Italy**: Tuscany and Umbria are known for their artisanal craftsmanship, especially in leather, ceramics, and textiles. Florence is a major centre for fashion and art, while rural areas are home to thriving local markets for gourmet food products and traditional crafts.
- **Southern Italy**: Southern regions like Sicily, Calabria, and Puglia are characterised by their agricultural economy, with a focus on food and wine. Artisanal goods, especially those that reflect the region's cultural heritage, are popular in local markets. Southern Italy also has a growing demand for organic and eco-friendly products.

4.3 Sustainability and Eco-Friendly Goods

Sustainability is an important factor for Italian consumers, particularly in urban areas. There is a growing demand for products that are environmentally friendly, ethically sourced, and made with sustainable materials. This trend is especially prevalent in sectors like fashion, food, and beauty.

What Defines an Eco-Friendly Product?

- **Sustainable Materials**: Products made from recycled, organic, or sustainably sourced materials resonate with Italian consumers. Whether it's organic cotton clothing, eco-friendly beauty products, or reusable household items, there is a strong market for products that minimize environmental impact.
- **Zero-Waste Packaging**: Italians are increasingly concerned about waste, particularly when it comes to

packaging. Offering products in reusable or compostable packaging can be a key selling point. Reducing plastic waste is especially important, with many consumers favouring brands that use sustainable alternatives.

- **Ethical Production**: Transparency in the production process is important to Italian consumers. Products that are fair-trade certified, made in small batches, or produced in ethical working conditions are highly valued, particularly among younger buyers.

Where to Sell Sustainable Products

Eco-friendly products are well-suited for both online and physical markets. Specialized markets focusing on sustainability and green living are becoming more common in urban areas like Milan, Rome, and Bologna. Additionally, online platforms like **Greenweez** and **EcoBio** cater to eco-conscious consumers looking for sustainable alternatives.

Chapter 4 - Summary

Selling in Italy offers exciting opportunities across a range of product categories, from luxury fashion to artisanal goods and gourmet food. By understanding the local market, adapting to regional and seasonal trends, and embracing the growing demand for sustainability, you can position your products for success in Italy. Whether you're selling at markets, through boutique stores, or online, tailoring your offerings to Italian tastes and values will help you thrive in this vibrant and diverse marketplace.

CHAPTER 5: SELLING INDUSTRIAL PRODUCTS AND SERVICES IN ITALY

Italy's industrial sector is one of the most advanced and diverse in Europe, known for its strong emphasis on manufacturing, engineering, automotive, and high-tech industries. While Italy is famous for fashion, food, and luxury goods, its industrial base - particularly in the northern regions - is a key driver of the country's economy. Selling industrial products and services in Italy requires a deep understanding of its industrial landscape, regulatory environment, and market expectations.

This chapter will provide insights into the industrial sectors in Italy, the strategies for entering this market, and how to navigate the specific challenges that come with selling industrial goods and services.

5.1 Key Industrial Sectors in Italy

Italy is a powerhouse in various industrial sectors, each with its own unique demands and opportunities. Understanding the most significant industries will help you target the right market and tailor your offerings accordingly.

Manufacturing and Engineering

- **Overview**: Manufacturing is a cornerstone of Italy's industrial sector, with a focus on precision engineering, machinery, and equipment. Italy is renowned for its production of industrial machinery used in sectors such as food processing, automotive, textiles, and packaging. The country is also a leading producer of robotics and automation systems.

- **Key Regions**: The northern regions, particularly **Lombardy**, **Veneto**, and **Emilia-Romagna**, are home to many of Italy's leading manufacturing companies. These regions are known for their advanced manufacturing hubs, producing high-quality industrial machinery and components.
- **Opportunities**: If you're selling industrial machinery or equipment, the demand for automation, innovation, and efficiency is growing across various sectors, particularly in food processing, automotive, and textile industries. Italian companies are looking to modernize their production lines, making this a promising market for automation solutions and cutting-edge technologies.

Automotive

- **Overview**: Italy is home to some of the world's most iconic automotive brands, including **Ferrari**, **Lamborghini**, and **Fiat**. The automotive industry in Italy is not only about producing luxury vehicles but also about manufacturing high-quality automotive components, parts, and industrial machinery used in car production.
- **Key Regions**: The **Piedmont** region, particularly the city of Turin, is the heart of Italy's automotive industry. Major automotive manufacturers, suppliers, and research centres are concentrated in this area.
- **Opportunities**: Companies that provide components, machinery, or services related to automotive manufacturing can find significant opportunities in Italy. Whether you're selling parts, engineering services, or automotive technologies, Italian manufacturers are looking for innovative and efficient solutions to stay competitive in the global market.

Renewable Energy and Environmental Technologies

- **Overview**: Italy is actively investing in renewable energy and environmental sustainability. The country has ambitious goals to increase the share of renewable energy sources, particularly in solar, wind, and hydroelectric power. Italy's focus on green technologies also extends to energy efficiency solutions for industrial processes.
- **Key Regions**: Renewable energy projects are spread throughout Italy, with major initiatives in regions like **Puglia**, **Sicily**, and **Lazio**. Northern Italy is also a key area for developing energy efficiency technologies for industrial use.
- **Opportunities**: If you're selling renewable energy solutions, energy-efficient machinery, or environmental consulting services, Italy presents a growing market. Industrial companies in Italy are looking to reduce their carbon footprint, optimise energy use, and comply with EU environmental regulations, creating opportunities for energy-efficient technologies and services.

Textiles and Fashion Production

- **Overview**: Italy's textile industry is world-renowned, with its focus on producing high-quality fabrics, clothing, and accessories. The country is a global leader in luxury fashion production, and behind every successful fashion brand is an advanced industrial sector producing the raw materials, textiles, and machinery needed for clothing production.
- **Key Regions**: **Tuscany** and **Lombardy** are the primary regions for textile manufacturing, while **Prato** is considered one of the largest textile districts in Europe.
- **Opportunities**: Companies that provide textile machinery, dyes, and fabrics, as well as manufacturing services, can tap into Italy's textile sector. Italian

manufacturers are looking for innovations in textile production, including sustainable and eco-friendly technologies.

5.2 Entering the Industrial Market in Italy

Selling industrial products and services in Italy requires more than just offering quality products - it demands an understanding of the business culture, procurement processes, and the local regulatory environment.

Research and Market Entry Strategy

- **Market Research**: Before entering the Italian industrial market, conduct thorough research on your specific sector, identifying key players, competitors, and market trends. Understanding local demand, pricing strategies, and procurement cycles is essential for creating a strong market entry strategy.
- **Industry Networks**: Joining industry associations, attending trade fairs, and building a local network of contacts can help you navigate the market and establish credibility. Italy has numerous trade fairs dedicated to industrial sectors, such as **SMAU** (technology), **Marmomac** (stone and machinery), and **Fiera Milano** (machinery and manufacturing).

Choosing the Right Distribution Model

Deciding how to distribute your products or services is a critical part of entering the Italian market. There are several approaches, depending on your goals and resources.

- **Direct Sales**: If you have a strong sales team and the resources to manage direct relationships with Italian buyers, this can be an effective model for selling high-value industrial products or services. Building direct relationships with key clients allows you to offer tailored solutions and negotiate long-term contracts.

- **Distributors and Agents**: Many international companies choose to partner with local distributors or sales agents who have deep market knowledge and established relationships with Italian industrial clients. This approach can help you enter the market more quickly, but it requires careful selection of partners who align with your business goals and brand.
- **Joint Ventures and Partnerships**: Partnering with Italian companies through joint ventures or strategic partnerships can provide access to local expertise, manufacturing facilities, or distribution networks. This approach is particularly useful for businesses looking to invest in long-term projects or industrial infrastructure.

5.3 Navigating Italian Industrial Regulations and Standards

Italy's industrial sector is subject to stringent regulations, particularly regarding quality, safety, and environmental standards. Understanding these regulations and ensuring compliance is crucial for selling industrial products and services in the country.

Certifications and Quality Standards

- **CE Marking**: For many industrial products, **CE marking** is mandatory, indicating that the product meets EU safety, health, and environmental protection standards. Ensuring that your products are CE certified is essential for legal compliance and market entry.
- **ISO Standards**: Italian industries often require compliance with **ISO standards** for quality management systems, environmental management, and safety protocols. Obtaining **ISO 9001** (quality management) or **ISO 14001** (environmental management) certification can enhance your credibility and make your products more appealing to Italian buyers.

Environmental and Safety Regulations

- **EU Directives**: Italy is part of the European Union, meaning that businesses must comply with EU regulations on industrial production, emissions, and waste management. Directives such as the **EU Waste Framework Directive** and **Industrial Emissions Directive** govern how industrial facilities manage environmental impact.

- **Occupational Health and Safety**: Italy enforces strict regulations on workplace safety, especially in industries like manufacturing and construction. Compliance with Italy's occupational health and safety laws is crucial to avoid penalties and ensure that your products or services meet industry expectations.

Procurement Processes

- **Public Procurement**: If you are selling industrial products or services to government entities or large corporations, understanding Italy's public procurement process is essential. Government contracts, particularly in sectors like infrastructure, energy, and transportation, are awarded through public tenders. These tenders often require compliance with specific standards and certifications.

- **Private Sector Procurement**: Italian private companies often rely on long-standing relationships with suppliers. Developing trust with buyers and proving the value and reliability of your products is crucial for securing contracts in the industrial sector.

5.4 Building Relationships with Italian Industrial Clients

Building strong relationships is critical to success in Italy's industrial sector. Italian business culture places

significant importance on personal connections, trust, and long-term partnerships.

Relationship Building in B2B Sales

- **Face-to-Face Meetings**: In the industrial sector, Italian buyers prefer face-to-face meetings to build trust and evaluate potential suppliers. While remote communication is becoming more common, in-person meetings are still highly valued, especially during the early stages of business relationships.
- **Networking and Industry Events**: Attending trade shows, conferences, and networking events is essential for connecting with key decision-makers in Italy's industrial sector. Building your reputation and networking with industry leaders can help establish your presence and open doors to new opportunities.

Trust and Long-Term Partnerships

- **Consistency and Reliability**: Italian industrial buyers are known for their preference for long-term partnerships with suppliers they trust. Focus on delivering consistent quality, meeting deadlines, and offering excellent after-sales support to strengthen these relationships.
- **Flexibility and Customisation**: Italian companies appreciate suppliers who can offer customised solutions tailored to their specific needs. Flexibility in product offerings, delivery times, and pricing can help you stand out and build a lasting partnership with your clients.

Chapter 5 - Summary

Selling industrial products and services in Italy presents significant opportunities across various sectors, from manufacturing and engineering to automotive and renewable energy. However, entering the market requires a solid understanding of Italy's industrial landscape, compliance with regulations, and a commitment to building long-term relationships. Whether you choose to enter the market through direct sales, partnerships, or distributors, success in Italy's industrial sector depends on your ability to offer high-quality, innovative solutions while navigating the country's unique business culture and regulatory environment.

By building trust with clients, ensuring compliance with local standards, and offering tailored solutions, you can position your business to thrive in Italy's competitive and dynamic industrial market.

CHAPTER 6: SELLING AT MARKETS AND FAIRS IN ITALY

Italy's markets and fairs are more than just places to buy and sell goods - they are integral to the country's cultural fabric. From the bustling street markets of Rome to the artisanal fairs of Tuscany, these venues offer entrepreneurs a unique opportunity to engage with consumers, showcase their products, and build relationships. Selling at markets in Italy allows you to connect with locals, tourists, and other vendors in a more personal way, giving your business an authentic, hands-on approach. In this chapter, we'll explore the types of markets in Italy, how to apply for a stall, and tips for maximising your sales.

6.1 Italy's Famous Markets

Italy is known for its vibrant and diverse markets, which vary greatly in size, frequency, and focus. Some markets specialize in food, others in fashion or antiques, and many feature a mix of goods. Understanding the different types of markets will help you choose the best venues to sell your products.

Weekly Markets (Mercati Settimanali)

- **What They Are**: Weekly markets are held in most Italian towns and cities, often in the main piazzas or market squares. These markets typically feature a range of goods, including fresh produce, clothing, household items, and handmade crafts. Many Italian families shop at their local weekly markets for everyday essentials, making these markets a key part of community life.

- **Where to Find Them**: Nearly every town in Italy hosts a weekly market, with larger markets in cities like Florence, Naples, and Rome. Examples include Florence's **San Lorenzo Market**, Rome's **Campo de' Fiori**, and Naples' **Mercato di Porta Nolana**.
- **What Sells**: Fashion, accessories, handmade crafts, and locally made food products are popular in weekly markets. Artisanal goods, such as leather products and jewellery, perform well in these markets, especially when they reflect local craftsmanship and heritage.

Flea Markets (Mercati delle Pulci)

- **What They Are**: Flea markets are popular in Italy, offering second-hand goods, vintage items, antiques, and curiosities. These markets attract collectors, bargain hunters, and tourists looking for unique finds. Flea markets can range from small, local events to large, city-wide gatherings.
- **Where to Find Them**: Some of the most famous flea markets in Italy include the **Mercato di Porta Portese** in Rome, one of the largest and oldest flea markets in the country, and Milan's **Fiera di Sinigaglia**, which offers a mix of vintage items, books, and handmade crafts.
- **What Sells**: Vintage clothing, retro furniture, antiques, second-hand goods, and collectible items. Flea market shoppers love discovering unique, one-of-a-kind items, so products with a vintage or handcrafted feel are ideal.

Artisanal Markets (Mercati Artigianali)

- **What They Are**: Artisanal markets focus on handmade goods and local craftsmanship. These markets are particularly popular in regions like Tuscany, where artisanal traditions are strong. They provide a great platform for selling unique, handcrafted items, from ceramics and leather goods to textiles and jewellery.

- **Where to Find Them**: Artisanal markets are common in cities and towns known for their craftsmanship, such as Florence, Siena, and Venice. Tuscany, in particular, has many artisanal markets where tourists and locals alike seek out high-quality handmade goods.
- **What Sells**: Handcrafted leather goods, ceramics, jewellery, and textiles. Products that are made using traditional methods or showcase local craftsmanship tend to perform well, as Italian consumers and tourists value authenticity and heritage.

Christmas Markets (Mercatini di Natale)

- **What They Are**: Christmas markets are festive, seasonal events held in towns and cities across Italy during the holiday season. These markets are known for their holiday-themed products, decorations, food, and gifts. They attract both locals and tourists looking to enjoy the holiday spirit and shop for unique gifts.
- **Where to Find Them**: Some of the most famous Christmas markets in Italy include the **Bolzano Christmas Market** in South Tyrol, the **Florence Christmas Market**, and the **Piazza Navona Christmas Market** in Rome. These markets are often held in scenic locations, adding to the festive atmosphere.
- **What Sells**: Handcrafted Christmas ornaments, holiday-themed gifts, artisanal foods, and seasonal decorations. Christmas markets are perfect for selling festive, high-quality products, particularly those with a handmade touch.

6.2 Setting Up a Stall: What You Need to Know

Selling at markets and fairs in Italy requires careful planning and preparation. From securing a spot at the market to designing an attractive stall, there are several factors to consider to ensure a successful experience.

Applying for a Stall

- **Market Permits**: Most markets in Italy require vendors to apply for a permit or stall space in advance. This process is usually managed by the local **Comune** (municipality) or the market organisers. Applications typically need to be submitted weeks or even months ahead of time, especially for popular markets and festivals.

- **Business Registration**: You will need to have a registered business in Italy, typically under a **Partita IVA**, to sell at markets. Ensure that you have the necessary permits and are registered with the local Chamber of Commerce if required.

- **Market Fees**: Stall fees vary depending on the location, size, and popularity of the market. Fees for small, local markets may be minimal, while high-profile events, such as Christmas markets or markets in major cities, may charge higher fees.

Designing Your Stall

- **Visual Appeal**: The appearance of your stall is crucial to attracting customers. Use bright, eye-catching colours that reflect your brand or product style. Consider investing in professional signage that clearly displays your brand name and what you sell.

- **Product Display**: How you display your products can significantly impact your sales. Use attractive displays that showcase your best products at eye level, and create a sense of organisation and abundance. Consider using decorative props or thematic elements that fit the style of your products, such as rustic wooden crates for artisanal goods or sleek stands for fashion items.

- **Lighting and Atmosphere**: If the market takes place in the evening or indoors, proper lighting is essential to making your stall stand out. Use battery-powered string lights or spotlights to highlight your products and create a warm, inviting atmosphere. Lighting can be a powerful tool for drawing customers in, especially at night markets or Christmas fairs.

What to Bring

- **Essential Equipment**: Make sure to bring everything you need to set up and run your stall smoothly, including tables, chairs, display stands, and packaging materials. Portable shelving units, tablecloths, and boxes for product storage can help you stay organized.
- **Payment Methods**: In Italy, many customers still prefer paying with cash at markets, but accepting card payments can give you a competitive edge. Mobile payment systems such as **SumUp** or **Zettle by PayPal** are widely used by market vendors and allow you to accept credit card payments using a mobile device.

6.3 Connecting with Customers in Person

Selling at markets gives you the unique opportunity to interact directly with your customers. Building rapport and creating a personal connection can significantly boost your sales and help you establish a loyal customer base.

Customer Engagement

- **Greet Your Customers**: Italians appreciate friendly, polite service, so be sure to greet potential customers with a warm smile and a simple **"Buongiorno"** or **"Buonasera"**. Make eye contact, but avoid being overly aggressive - let customers browse freely while being approachable.
- **Share the Story Behind Your Products**: Italian consumers, especially at artisanal and handmade

markets, love to know the story behind the products they are buying. If your goods are handcrafted or have a unique cultural or personal significance, share that story. Explain the materials used, the craftsmanship involved, and the inspiration behind your designs.

Negotiating and Offering Discounts

- **Haggling**: At some markets, particularly flea markets, haggling is common. Be prepared for customers to negotiate prices, and consider offering small discounts on bulk purchases or if a customer buys multiple items. However, for artisanal or high-end products, set a price that reflects the value of your craftsmanship, and be cautious about lowering it too much.
- **Seasonal Offers**: Offering seasonal promotions or special deals during market events can help boost sales. Consider offering a discount for repeat customers or including a small gift with purchases over a certain amount.

Building Relationships for Repeat Business

- **Collect Customer Information**: Markets offer a great opportunity to gather customer contact information. Encourage buyers to sign up for your newsletter or follow you on social media by offering a small discount or free sample. This allows you to keep in touch with customers and inform them about future markets or new product launches.
- **Customer Loyalty**: Building relationships with repeat customers is key to long-term success at markets. Make an effort to recognise returning customers and offer them special deals or incentives to encourage loyalty.

Chapter 6 - Summary

Selling at markets and fairs in Italy offers a unique and rewarding experience for entrepreneurs. Whether you're showcasing your products at a weekly market in Florence, a Christmas market in Bolzano, or an artisanal fair in Tuscany, markets allow you to connect directly with your customers and offer them an authentic experience. By understanding the different types of markets, securing the right permits, and creating an inviting stall, you can maximise your sales potential. Personal engagement, clear communication, and attention to detail will help you build lasting relationships with customers and succeed in Italy's vibrant marketplace.

CHAPTER 7: SELLING ONLINE IN ITALY

The rise of e-commerce in Italy presents an exciting opportunity for entrepreneurs looking to reach a broader audience beyond physical markets. Italian consumers are increasingly embracing online shopping, particularly in fashion, electronics, beauty, and food sectors. However, selling online in Italy comes with its own set of challenges and opportunities. This chapter will guide you through Italy's e-commerce landscape, how to build a localised marketing strategy, and the importance of offering secure payment methods and reliable shipping.

7.1 Italy's E-Commerce Landscape

Italy is one of Europe's fastest-growing e-commerce markets, with more consumers shopping online for convenience, better prices, and wider product selections. Understanding the e-commerce environment in Italy will help you tailor your strategy to succeed in this competitive space.

Popular E-Commerce Categories

Certain product categories dominate Italy's online shopping market. These include:

- **Fashion and Apparel**: Italians are known for their love of fashion, and this extends to online shopping. Clothing, shoes, accessories, and designer goods are all popular purchases. Italian consumers are particularly interested in finding exclusive or hard-to-find items online.
- **Electronics**: Smartphones, laptops, and home appliances are highly sought after in Italy's online

marketplace. Italian consumers often look online to compare prices and take advantage of deals on tech products.

- **Beauty and Wellness**: Skincare, cosmetics, and wellness products are experiencing significant growth online, particularly among younger consumers who prioritize convenience and access to a wider variety of brands.
- **Food and Beverages**: Italy's love of food extends into the digital space. Specialty foods, regional delicacies, wine, and organic products are popular online purchases, particularly for consumers looking for high-quality ingredients delivered to their door.

Key E-Commerce Platforms in Italy

To successfully sell online in Italy, you need to choose the right platform. While many entrepreneurs use their own e-commerce websites, there are also popular online marketplaces that provide ready-made solutions for reaching Italian consumers.

- **Amazon.it**: Amazon is the leading e-commerce platform in Italy, offering a wide range of products across various categories. Setting up a seller account on **Amazon.it** allows you to tap into a large and loyal customer base. Additionally, Amazon's **Fulfilment by Amazon (FBA)** service can handle storage, shipping, and customer service for you.
- **eBay Italia**: eBay remains a popular choice for both new and used goods in Italy. It is particularly useful for entrepreneurs selling second-hand items, vintage goods, or collectibles. eBay's platform provides a simple interface for selling and reaching customers across the country.
- **Etsy**: For sellers of handmade, vintage, or artisanal products, **Etsy** is a great platform. Italian consumers increasingly turn to Etsy to find unique, high-quality crafts, jewellery, and home decor items. It's an ideal

marketplace for sellers focusing on authenticity and craftsmanship.

- **Zalando**: As one of Europe's largest fashion-focused platforms, **Zalando** is an excellent choice for selling clothing, shoes, and accessories. Zalando offers integration with a wide range of fashion brands and retailers, providing visibility in the competitive Italian fashion market.

- **Tannico**: For food and beverage entrepreneurs, particularly in the wine industry, **Tannico** is a leading e-commerce platform in Italy specializing in high-end wines. Selling on this platform can help you reach connoisseurs looking for premium products.

7.2 Crafting a Localised Marketing Strategy

To succeed in Italy's e-commerce market, your online store must be fully localised for Italian consumers. Italian buyers prefer websites that are in their native language, reflect local tastes and preferences, and offer familiar payment methods and customer service options.

Creating a User-Friendly Website in Italian

- **Italian Language**: The most critical step in localising your e-commerce business for Italy is translating your website into Italian. Even though many Italians speak English, they are much more likely to shop on a site that communicates in their native language. Invest in professional translation services to ensure that your product descriptions, customer service pages, and checkout process are in clear and accurate Italian.

- **Cultural Sensitivity**: Italians value aesthetics and quality, so make sure your website reflects the sophistication and design sensibilities of Italian consumers. Clean layouts, beautiful imagery, and a strong focus on product quality will help attract Italian buyers. Avoid using overly aggressive sales tactics - Italians appreciate a more subtle approach.

Search Engine Optimisation (SEO) for the Italian Market

- **Local SEO**: Optimising your website for **Google.it** is essential for attracting Italian shoppers. Use Italian keywords in your product descriptions, blog posts, and meta tags to rank higher in local search results. Incorporating region-specific terms, such as **"artigianale"** (handmade) or **"biologico"** (organic), can help target niche markets.

- **Keyword Research**: Use tools like **Google Keyword Planner** or **Ubersuggest** to identify popular search terms that Italian consumers are using to find products in your industry. Craft your website's content to naturally incorporate these keywords and phrases.

Social Media Marketing

Social media is an essential tool for reaching Italian consumers, who are highly active on platforms like Instagram, Facebook, and Pinterest. Using social media to showcase your products and engage with your audience can significantly boost your brand's visibility in Italy.

- **Instagram**: Italians love Instagram for fashion, lifestyle, and beauty inspiration. Use Instagram to showcase high-quality photos and videos of your products, and take advantage of features like Instagram Stories and Instagram Shopping to create a direct path to purchase.

- **Facebook**: Facebook remains a widely used platform in Italy, making it a good choice for running targeted ad campaigns. You can create Facebook Ads tailored to specific demographics, interests, and regions in Italy, allowing you to reach the right audience.

- **Pinterest**: If you're selling products in categories like home decor, fashion, or crafts, Pinterest can be a powerful platform for driving traffic to your website. Italian users turn to Pinterest for inspiration, so creating visually appealing pins that link back to your store can generate both brand awareness and sales.

7.3 Payment Methods and Security

Italian consumers value security and convenience when shopping online, so offering familiar and trusted payment methods is crucial for increasing conversion rates. Additionally, ensuring that your website complies with local regulations will build trust with Italian shoppers.

Preferred Payment Methods in Italy

- **Credit and Debit Cards (Carta di Credito/Debito)**: Most Italian consumers use **credit and debit cards**, with popular networks like **Visa, Mastercard,** and **American Express**. It's essential to integrate these payment options into your e-commerce platform.
- **PayPal**: PayPal is widely trusted in Italy for online payments. Many consumers prefer it for its simplicity and security. If you're selling online in Italy, enabling PayPal as a payment method will likely increase your sales.
- **Bank Transfers (Bonifico Bancario)**: Although less common, some Italian consumers still prefer to pay via bank transfer, particularly for larger or more expensive purchases. Offering this option can help you cater to a broader audience.
- **Cash on Delivery (Contrassegno)**: In Italy, some customers still prefer **cash on delivery** as a payment option. While this is less common in major cities, offering it as a payment method for certain product categories or regions could boost your sales.

Ensuring Secure Transactions

- **SSL Certificates**: Italian consumers are particularly concerned about security when shopping online. Make sure your website has a valid **SSL certificate** (indicated by the "https" in your website URL), which ensures that customer data is encrypted during transactions.

- **GDPR Compliance**: Italy, as part of the European Union, requires all businesses to comply with the **General Data Protection Regulation (GDPR)**. Ensure that your website clearly informs customers about how their data will be used, and provide an option for them to manage or withdraw consent. Non-compliance with GDPR can result in hefty fines.

7.4 Shipping and Logistics for Online Sellers

Reliable shipping and efficient logistics are key to building a successful e-commerce business in Italy. Italian consumers expect fast and reliable delivery, and clear return policies can boost customer satisfaction and encourage repeat business.

Shipping Options

- **Poste Italiane**: Italy's national postal service, **Poste Italiane**, offers a range of shipping options for domestic and international deliveries. **Pacco Ordinario** is a cost-effective choice for standard shipping, while **Posta Celere** provides express delivery for time-sensitive orders.

- **Private Couriers**: For faster or more reliable shipping, private couriers like **DHL**, **UPS**, and **FedEx** offer more advanced logistics solutions. These companies provide tracking services and often offer faster shipping options, which are ideal for e-commerce businesses shipping larger quantities or fragile items.

- **Click-and-Collect Services**: Some Italian consumers prefer to pick up their purchases at local collection points rather than having them delivered to their homes. If you have a physical store or partner with local retailers, offering a **click-and-collect** option can provide customers with greater flexibility.

Managing Returns

- **Return Policies**: Italian consumer protection laws guarantee the right to return most goods purchased online within 14 days of receipt. Clearly state your return policy on your website, and make the return process as simple as possible for your customers. Offering free returns, when feasible, can help you build trust with Italian shoppers.
- **Handling Refunds**: Make sure that your refund process is smooth and customer-friendly. Fast and hassle-free refunds are essential for building loyalty and increasing customer satisfaction.

Chapter 7 - Summary

Selling online in Italy offers exciting opportunities to reach a larger, tech-savvy audience. By choosing the right e-commerce platforms, creating a fully localized shopping experience, and offering secure, trusted payment options, you can position your online store for success in Italy. Efficient logistics and transparent return policies will further enhance customer satisfaction, helping you build a loyal customer base. As e-commerce continues to grow in Italy, staying ahead of consumer trends and optimising your online store for local preferences will give you a competitive edge.

CHAPTER 8: MARKETING STRATEGIES FOR ITALIAN CONSUMERS

Marketing to Italian consumers requires a deep understanding of their cultural values, buying behaviours, and preferences. Italian consumers are discerning, placing a high value on quality, craftsmanship, and authenticity. They also appreciate strong aesthetics and a well-told story behind a product. To successfully market your products in Italy, you need to craft a strategy that resonates with these core values while leveraging the right marketing channels to reach your audience.

In this chapter, we'll explore how to tailor your marketing efforts to Italian consumers, focusing on messaging, digital marketing strategies, social media, and email marketing. You'll also learn how to engage with influencers and build customer loyalty through effective communication and personalisation.

8.1 Understanding the Italian Buyer Persona

Italian consumers are known for their sophistication and their strong sense of style. They prioritise quality, attention to detail, and tradition. Understanding these traits and how they influence buying decisions is key to crafting your marketing messages.

The Importance of Quality and Craftsmanship

Italian consumers take pride in the quality of the products they buy. Whether it's fashion, food, or home decor, products that showcase craftsmanship, heritage, and durability are highly valued. When marketing your products to Italians, emphasise these qualities and highlight the artisanal elements of your products, especially if they are handmade or locally produced.

- **Messaging Tip**: Use phrases like **"artigianale"** (handmade), **"fatto a mano"** (handcrafted), or **"qualità eccellente"** (excellent quality) in your marketing materials to convey the craftsmanship and attention to detail behind your products.

Sustainability and Ethical Values

Sustainability is becoming increasingly important in Italy, particularly among younger, urban consumers. Products that are eco-friendly, sustainably sourced, or ethically produced resonate well with Italian buyers who care about the environment and social responsibility. If your business prioritises sustainability, make sure this is a key part of your brand messaging.

- **Messaging Tip**: Highlight your sustainable practices, such as eco-friendly packaging, fair-trade sourcing, or carbon-neutral shipping. Use terms like **"biologico"** (organic) or **"sostenibile"** (sustainable) to appeal to environmentally conscious consumers.

Aesthetics and Storytelling

Italian consumers are drawn to products with a strong aesthetic appeal and a compelling story. Italians have a deep appreciation for art, design, and beauty, so your branding, packaging, and product presentation should reflect this. Telling the story behind your brand—whether it's the process of creating your products or the inspiration behind them—helps build an emotional connection with Italian buyers.

- **Messaging Tip**: Use storytelling to convey the journey of your products. Whether it's the artisans who make them or the inspiration behind their design, sharing these stories through social media, your website, or even on product packaging can enhance their perceived value.

8.2 Effective Advertising Channels in Italy

To reach Italian consumers, it's essential to use the right advertising channels. Italians are highly active on social media and spend a significant amount of time online, making digital marketing a powerful tool. However, traditional advertising methods like print and television can still be effective, especially for reaching older demographics or promoting luxury goods.

Digital Advertising

- **Google Ads**: Search engine marketing (SEM) via **Google Ads** is an effective way to reach Italian consumers who are actively searching for products online. By targeting relevant keywords in Italian, you can drive traffic to your website or online store. Localised ads that reflect Italian cultural references or regional preferences can increase your ad performance.
- **Social Media Ads**: Italians are highly active on platforms like Instagram, Facebook, and YouTube. Social media advertising allows you to reach a wide audience with highly targeted ads based on location, interests, and purchasing behaviour. Using **Instagram Ads** or **Facebook Ads**, for example, you can showcase your products through visually appealing images or videos that align with Italian tastes.

Influencer Marketing

Influencer marketing is particularly effective in Italy, where consumers trust recommendations from influencers, especially in sectors like fashion, beauty, food, and travel. Partnering with Italian influencers can help you build credibility and reach new audiences.

- **Micro-Influencers**: While partnering with major influencers can be impactful, micro-influencers (those with smaller but highly engaged followings) are often more trusted and relatable. Collaborating with influencers who align with your brand's values can help you gain exposure to niche markets and build trust with their followers.

- **Instagram Takeovers**: Consider hosting an **Instagram takeover**, where an Italian influencer temporarily takes control of your account to showcase your products and connect with your followers. This can drive engagement and give your brand a more personal touch.

Traditional Media

- **Print and TV Advertising**: Traditional media, such as print and television, remains relevant in Italy, particularly for promoting luxury goods, high-end fashion, or artisanal products. Advertising in well-known fashion magazines like **Vogue Italia** or on television channels such as **Rai** or **Mediaset** can enhance your brand's prestige and reach a wider, more diverse audience.

8.3 Building Customer Trust and Loyalty

In Italy, trust and long-term relationships are crucial for building a loyal customer base. Italian consumers are selective about the brands they support, and businesses that focus on delivering exceptional service, quality, and transparency can earn lasting loyalty.

Transparency and Clear Communication

Italian consumers value honesty and clarity in their interactions with brands. Be transparent about your product's origins, materials, and pricing. Ensure that your website, product descriptions, and customer service communication are clear, concise, and accurate.

- **Product Information**: Provide detailed product descriptions that highlight quality, craftsmanship, and any special attributes like organic or sustainable materials. Be upfront about shipping costs, return policies, and delivery times to avoid any misunderstandings.

Personalisation and Tailored Marketing

Personalised marketing is highly effective in Italy. Tailoring your communication to each customer's preferences can improve engagement and drive sales. Italians appreciate businesses that make an effort to personalise their shopping experience, whether through customised product recommendations or exclusive offers.

- **Email Marketing**: Use email marketing to build and maintain relationships with your customers. Personalised email campaigns featuring product recommendations based on past purchases, special promotions, or invitations to exclusive events can enhance customer loyalty.
- **VIP Programs**: Offering loyalty programs or VIP memberships to your most loyal customers can help foster long-term relationships. Consider offering special discounts, early access to new products, or invitations to exclusive events for repeat buyers.

Leveraging Customer Reviews and Testimonials

Customer reviews are an essential trust-building tool in Italy, where word of mouth and recommendations play a significant role in purchasing decisions. Encourage satisfied customers to leave reviews on your website or social media pages and consider featuring testimonials prominently on your website.

- **Review Platforms**: Encourage reviews on popular platforms like **Trustpilot**, **Google Reviews**, or **Facebook Reviews**. Be sure to respond to reviews—both positive and negative—in a professional and respectful manner.

8.4 Social Media and Email Marketing for Italian Consumers

In the digital age, social media and email marketing are two of the most powerful tools for reaching Italian consumers and keeping them engaged with your brand. Here's how to optimise your strategies for these platforms.

Social Media Strategy

- **Instagram**: As one of Italy's most popular social platforms, Instagram is ideal for showcasing visually appealing products such as fashion, beauty, and lifestyle goods. Italians appreciate high-quality photography and videos, so invest in professional visuals that reflect your brand's aesthetic. Make use of **Instagram Stories**, **Reels**, and **Instagram Shopping** to create an engaging and interactive experience for your followers.

- **Facebook**: Facebook remains an important platform for reaching a broader audience in Italy. Use **Facebook Ads** to target specific demographics based on location, interests, and behaviours. Regularly post updates, product announcements, and behind-the-scenes content to keep your followers engaged.

- **Pinterest**: Italians use Pinterest to discover and save ideas for fashion, home decor, and DIY projects. For sellers of fashion, home goods, or crafts, Pinterest is an excellent platform for driving traffic to your online store through **Pinterest Pins** that link directly to product pages.

Email Marketing Strategy

- **Personalised Campaigns**: Italian consumers respond well to personalised email campaigns. Segment your email list based on customer preferences, purchase history, or geographical location to send tailored content that resonates with each group. Use personalised subject lines and content to increase open and click-through rates.

- **Exclusive Offers**: Offering exclusive discounts, early access to sales, or personalised product recommendations via email can help you build loyalty and encourage repeat purchases. Italian consumers appreciate special treatment and are more likely to respond to email campaigns that make them feel valued.

- **Seasonal Promotions**: Create email campaigns around Italian holidays or seasonal events, such as **Ferragosto** (August vacation season) or Christmas. Highlight how your products are perfect for these occasions, and offer time-limited discounts to create urgency.

Chapter 8 - Summary

Marketing to Italian consumers requires a thoughtful and tailored approach that emphasises quality, craftsmanship, and authenticity. By understanding the values and preferences of Italian buyers, you can craft marketing messages that resonate with their love of style, sustainability, and storytelling. Leveraging the right advertising channels, from social media to influencer partnerships and email marketing, will help you build brand awareness and engage with Italian consumers on a deeper level. Ultimately, fostering trust, offering personalised experiences, and maintaining clear communication are key to building long-term customer loyalty in the Italian market.

CHAPTER 9: NAVIGATING CULTURAL AND BUSINESS ETIQUETTE

Understanding Italian business culture and social etiquette is crucial for building strong relationships and conducting business successfully in Italy. Italians place great value on personal connections, formality, and clear communication in professional settings. Whether you're meeting potential partners, negotiating deals, or engaging with customers, your ability to respect and adapt to Italian customs will play a significant role in your success.

In this chapter, we'll explore the key aspects of Italian business etiquette, including how to address people, conduct meetings, and build relationships with clients and partners. We'll also provide tips on navigating social and business interactions effectively.

9.1 The Importance of Punctuality and Precision

Punctuality is valued in Italian business culture, but there is some flexibility depending on the region and context. Italians are generally known for their relaxed approach to time in social settings, but in business, arriving late can still be seen as unprofessional, particularly in the northern regions.

Being on Time

- **Meetings and Appointments**: In business settings, especially in the northern cities like Milan, Turin, and Venice, punctuality is essential. Arriving on time shows respect for the other party's schedule and reflects your professionalism. However, in more relaxed southern regions such as Sicily and Calabria, there may be a bit more leniency, and being a few minutes late is generally acceptable.

- **Notifying in Advance**: If you are running late for any reason, it is courteous to notify your Italian counterparts as soon as possible. A brief phone call or text explaining the delay is often appreciated and helps maintain a positive relationship.

Precision in Communication

Italians appreciate clarity and precision in business discussions. Ensure that your proposals and presentations are well-organised and backed by data. Italians enjoy in-depth conversations and may expect you to explain your ideas thoroughly, so be prepared to engage in detailed discussions.

- **Follow-Up**: After meetings, it's a good practice to follow up with a summary email that outlines the main points discussed and any agreed-upon next steps. This helps keep everyone on the same page and reinforces your professionalism.

9.2 Formal vs. Informal Interactions

Italian business culture tends to be more formal than in many other countries, particularly in the early stages of a professional relationship. Knowing when to use formal or informal language and how to address colleagues or clients appropriately is key to making a good impression.

Using Titles and Formal Address

- **Titles Matter**: Italians place importance on titles, and it's common to address people using their professional or academic titles, such as **Dottore** (Doctor) or **Ingegnere** (Engineer), followed by their last name. If someone has a title, use it unless they invite you to address them by their first name.

- **Formal vs. Informal Language**: In initial business meetings, it's appropriate to use the formal **"Lei"** when addressing someone, as it shows respect. Over time, as the relationship becomes more familiar, your Italian counterparts may suggest switching to the informal **"tu"**. Wait for this cue before making the switch.

Dress Code

- **Business Attire**: Italians are known for their impeccable sense of style, and this extends to business settings. For men, this usually means a well-tailored suit, while women are expected to dress stylishly in business-appropriate clothing. Even in more casual environments, Italians still prioritize looking polished and put together.

- **Casual Settings**: In more relaxed or creative industries, such as fashion or tech, the dress code may be less formal. However, even in casual settings, Italians prefer to dress elegantly and with attention to detail. Avoid overly casual or sloppy attire, as appearance is still considered a reflection of professionalism.

9.3 Conducting Meetings in Italy

Meetings in Italy can be both formal and social. Italians like to establish personal connections before getting into business discussions, so it's important to approach meetings with both professionalism and a sense of warmth.

Preparing for the Meeting

- **Agenda**: Meetings in Italy typically follow a clear agenda, but don't expect a strict, time-limited structure. Italians prefer to take their time discussing ideas and often encourage open dialogue. Be prepared for longer discussions, particularly if your meeting involves brainstorming or negotiations.

- **Materials and Presentations**: Bring well-prepared

materials, including printed copies of any proposals, presentations, or data you plan to discuss. Italians appreciate thoroughness and attention to detail, so ensure that your information is well-researched and easy to follow.

During the Meeting

- **Politeness and Formality**: Meetings typically begin with formal greetings and small talk, which helps to establish rapport before diving into business matters. Shake hands firmly, make eye contact, and greet your counterparts with **"Buongiorno"** (Good morning) or **"Buonasera"** (Good evening), depending on the time of day.

- **Debating Ideas**: Italian business culture values lively debate and intellectual discussions. Don't be afraid to present your ideas confidently, but also be prepared for others to challenge them. Italians enjoy exploring different perspectives and may ask probing questions to fully understand your point of view.

- **Decision-Making**: Decision-making in Italy can be a deliberate process, often involving multiple stakeholders. Italian businesspeople tend to be thorough and cautious, particularly when making long-term commitments. Be patient and allow time for your counterparts to consult with colleagues or superiors before finalising agreements.

Ending the Meeting

- **Summarise Key Points**: Before concluding the meeting, it's common to summarise the main points discussed and outline the next steps. This ensures that everyone is on the same page and understands their responsibilities moving forward.

- **Follow-Up**: Sending a follow-up email after the meeting is a standard practice. In your email, reiterate the key points discussed, confirm any agreements, and outline the next steps. This not only shows professionalism but also keeps the conversation moving forward.

9.4 Building Relationships with Italian Clients and Partners

Relationships are central to doing business in Italy. Italians value trust and personal connections, and they prefer to work with people they know and respect. Building a solid relationship with your Italian counterparts can open doors to long-term business success.

The Importance of Trust

- **Consistency and Reliability**: Italian businesspeople place a high value on trustworthiness and reliability. Delivering on promises, meeting deadlines, and maintaining clear communication are essential for building a solid reputation. If you gain their trust, Italian partners and clients are likely to remain loyal to your business in the long term.
- **Transparency**: Italians appreciate honesty and transparency in business dealings. Be open about your intentions, pricing, and any potential challenges. Transparency helps to establish trust and prevents misunderstandings down the line.

Networking and Socialising

- **Networking Events**: Attending networking events, industry conferences, and trade fairs is a valuable way to build relationships with Italian clients and partners. Italians enjoy socialising and discussing business in informal settings, so attending these events can help you form connections that extend beyond the office.
- **Socialising After Hours**: Italians often combine business with social activities. Business lunches,

dinners, and even coffee meetings are common ways to discuss business in a more relaxed atmosphere. However, avoid discussing business matters too quickly—allow the conversation to flow naturally, and wait for your host to bring up business topics.

9.5 Business Gifts and Etiquette

Gift-giving is not a common practice in Italian business culture, but there are certain occasions when offering a small gift may be appropriate. Understanding when and how to give gifts can help you navigate these situations with grace.

When to Give a Gift

- **Client Relationships**: Small, thoughtful gifts may be given during the holiday season or to mark the successful completion of a project. Gifts should be tasteful and not too extravagant, as excessive gifts may be seen as inappropriate or even as a bribe.

- **Business Partners**: If you have established a long-term partnership, a symbolic gift that reflects your appreciation and the cultural background of your country may be welcomed. However, avoid giving anything too personal or lavish.

Gift-Giving Tips

- **Cultural Sensitivity**: When choosing a gift, ensure that it aligns with Italian cultural values and avoids any potential misunderstandings. For example, avoid gifts like overly promotional items or anything that could be perceived as too personal.

- **Presentation**: Italians appreciate elegance and attention to detail, so take care in how you present your gift. Wrap the gift beautifully, and consider presenting it at the end of a meeting or social event.

Chapter 9 - Summary

Understanding Italian business etiquette is crucial for building strong, lasting relationships with clients, partners, and colleagues. By respecting the importance of punctuality, formality, and trust, you can create a positive impression and establish credibility in the Italian business world. Socialising, networking, and following up after meetings are all key elements of maintaining professional relationships in Italy. Navigating cultural nuances and demonstrating respect for Italian customs will help you succeed in the Italian market, both professionally and personally.

CHAPTER 10: CONCLUSION: EMBRACE THE OPPORTUNITY IN ITALY

Italy is a land of opportunity for entrepreneurs and travellers alike. From its rich cultural heritage to its thriving markets, Italy offers an environment that values quality, craftsmanship, and authenticity. Whether you're selling fashion, artisanal goods, gourmet food, or luxury products, the Italian marketplace rewards businesses that are adaptable, creative, and deeply attuned to local values.

In this final chapter, we will reflect on the key insights you've learned throughout this guide and explore the next steps you can take to fully embrace the opportunity of travelling and selling in Italy.

10.1 Reflecting on the Journey

Throughout this guide, we've explored every aspect of what it takes to travel and sell in Italy, from understanding regional differences and managing logistics, to mastering business etiquette and navigating the online marketplace. By now, you should have a clear picture of how to approach your business in Italy and connect with Italian consumers in meaningful ways.

Key Takeaways

- **Cultural Appreciation is Essential**: Italy's rich cultural diversity means that every region has its own customs, traditions, and consumer preferences. To succeed, you must tailor your approach to match these nuances, whether you're selling luxury goods in Milan, artisanal products in Florence, or gourmet foods in Sicily.

- **Markets and E-Commerce are Vital Channels**: Italy's vibrant street markets, fairs, and festivals offer a fantastic opportunity to engage with consumers face-to-face. At the same time, e-commerce continues to grow rapidly, allowing you to reach a wider audience. Whether you prefer in-person selling or online platforms, Italy offers a range of sales channels to suit your business model.

- **Relationships and Trust Drive Success**: Italians value personal relationships in both business and life. Building trust and establishing strong personal connections with clients, partners, and customers will be key to your long-term success in Italy. Consistency, reliability, and transparency are all essential elements of gaining the loyalty of Italian consumers.

- **Adaptability is Key**: Whether you're navigating Italy's bustling urban centres or its more relaxed rural towns, flexibility is essential. Each region offers different opportunities and challenges, so staying adaptable and willing to learn from the local culture will help you thrive.

10.2 Moving Forward: Actionable Steps

Now that you have a comprehensive understanding of the Italian market, it's time to put your knowledge into action. Whether you're launching a new venture or expanding an existing business, here are some practical steps to help you move forward.

1. Choose Your Business Structure and Register

- If you haven't already, decide on the most suitable business structure for your venture. Whether it's the **Partita IVA** for small entrepreneurs or a more formal structure like an **SRL**, ensure that you have all the necessary legal registrations in place. This will allow you to operate smoothly and comply with Italy's tax and business regulations.

2. Refine Your Product Offering

- Take a close look at your product lineup and consider how it fits with Italian consumer preferences. Are your products aligned with Italy's love for quality, craftsmanship, and sustainability? Tailor your product descriptions, packaging, and branding to appeal to Italian tastes, focusing on storytelling and attention to detail.

3. Build Your Online Presence

- If you're planning to sell online, ensure that your website is fully optimised for Italian consumers. Translate your site into Italian, integrate localized SEO strategies, and offer familiar payment options like **Carta di Credito**, **PayPal**, and **Bonifico Bancario**. Consider running targeted social media campaigns to reach Italian audiences, particularly on platforms like Instagram and Facebook.

4. Explore Market Opportunities

- Identify the markets, fairs, and festivals that align with your product category and start applying for stalls or participation. Research local events in key cities and regions where your products are likely to resonate, and tailor your approach to each market's unique audience.

5. Cultivate Relationships

- Focus on building strong, personal relationships with Italian clients, partners, and suppliers. Attend networking events, industry conferences, and trade shows to meet potential collaborators and build your reputation in the Italian business community.

10.3 Embracing the Adventure of Entrepreneurship in Italy

Travelling and selling in Italy isn't just about running a business - it's about embracing a way of life. Italy's culture, beauty, and traditions provide a unique backdrop for entrepreneurship, allowing you to combine business with the joy of discovery.

The Rewards of Travelling and Selling

- **Cultural Immersion**: By travelling through Italy and selling at local markets or stores, you'll experience Italy's regional diversity firsthand. Whether it's the elegance of Milan's fashion scene or the artisanal charm of Tuscany's markets, each place offers its own rich experiences and opportunities.
- **A Global Brand**: Establishing a presence in Italy can elevate your brand on a global scale. Italy is known for its influence in fashion, design, food, and luxury goods. If you can succeed in this discerning market, your brand will be seen as one that meets the highest standards of quality and craftsmanship, opening doors to other European markets and beyond.
- **Flexibility and Freedom**: Running a business while travelling offers the freedom to explore, grow, and adapt. You'll have the flexibility to move between cities, participate in new markets, and evolve your brand as you experience different regions of Italy.

10.4 Final Words of Encouragement

Selling in Italy is both a challenge and an incredible opportunity. Success in this market requires a deep understanding of the culture, a respect for tradition, and the ability to adapt to local preferences. But if you approach it with passion, creativity, and perseverance, Italy offers immense rewards.

Remember that building a business in Italy is a journey. Whether you're selling handmade crafts at a local market, launching an e-commerce site, or establishing partnerships with Italian retailers, take the time to learn from every experience. With each step, you'll grow more confident in navigating the intricacies of the Italian market.

Italy is a place where beauty, quality, and tradition converge. By embracing these values and bringing your own unique vision to the market, you can create a lasting impact and build a successful business in one of the world's most culturally rich and diverse countries.

So go forward with confidence. Embrace the challenge, seize the opportunity, and let your entrepreneurial journey in Italy begin.

Appendices

Useful Resources for Entrepreneurs in Italy

- **Chambers of Commerce (Camera di Commercio)**: The local Chamber of Commerce can provide valuable resources for entrepreneurs, including information on registering a business, finding market opportunities, and networking events.
- **Agenzia delle Entrate**: Italy's Revenue Agency provides guidance on VAT registration, tax compliance, and business filings. Website: www.agenziaentrate.gov.it
- **ICE (Italian Trade Agency)**: The Italian Trade Agency offers support to entrepreneurs looking to export products or enter the Italian market. Website: www.ice.it

Important Websites

- **Amazon Italy**: www.amazon.it – For setting up an online store on Amazon's Italian platform.

- **Etsy Italy**: www.etsy.com/it – For selling handmade and vintage products to Italian customers.
- **Zalando**: www.zalando.it – For selling fashion and accessories to Italian consumers.
- **Poste Italiane**: www.poste.it – For handling shipping and logistics within Italy.

Chapter 10 - Summary

Italy offers vast opportunities for entrepreneurs ready to embrace its culture, consumer preferences, and business landscape. Whether you're selling online or in-person, the Italian market rewards quality, creativity, and authenticity. With a clear understanding of the regional differences, market trends, and business etiquette, you can confidently take the next steps toward building a successful business in Italy. Enjoy the adventure, build lasting relationships, and unlock the full potential of travelling and selling in this remarkable country.

ABOUT THE AUTHOR

J K Lewis

J K Lewis has spent the past 30 years working, travelling and successfully selling in countries all around the world. He has lived in the UK, Germany and in South Korea; business has taken him all around Europe, the US and America, Asia and the MEA region. His sales and marketing experience covers a wide range of Products  and Services, from High-value German Engineering, to UK made special machinery, American Quality Management Services, to Chinese packaging and labels.

www.ingramcontent.com/pod-product-compliance
Lightning Source LLC
Chambersburg PA
CBHW070210230526
45471CB00002B/909